MacOS Catalina for Seniors

The Simple Manual to Operate Your Mac

Alec Young

TABLE OF CONTENT

Introduction

The macOS Catalina which was launched in October 2019, is the latest operating system for the Apple Mac family. The new software brought with it several new exciting features that may seem overwhelming even to existing users. Some of these features include the Screen Time, division of iTunes into 3 separate apps, using the iPad as a second screen, otherwise known as Sidecar and lots more.

This user guide contains detailed steps on how to explore all the new features on your computer along with screenshots to make it easy for you to familiarize yourself with the workings of the macOS Catalina. Whether you are just buying a new Mac device or downloading the new software to your existing device, this book would help you to achieve better and faster productivity.

If you have any of the following Mac computers, you would be able to download and enjoy all the new features that come with the macOS Catalina:

- MacBook Air (2012 or newer)
- MacBook (2015 or newer)
- Mac mini (2012 or newer)
- MacBook Pro (2012 or newer)
- iMac Pro (2017 or newer)
- iMac (2012 or newer)
- Mac Pro (2013 or newer)

No More iTunes

iTunes has now been broken into three apps: Podcasts, Music and TV app. While these apps are similar to iTunes in function, they are still different in the features. If you are wondering how you can manage your devices on the new macOS Catalina, worry not, as you can still do this using the Finder on your computer instead of the app. The Music app gives you full access to the music library, just like you have in iTunes, irrespective of whether you purchased the songs or copied from a CD. The Podcast app is especially useful to lovers of podcasts. Rather than going into iTunes to access your Podcast, the Podcast now has its own apps where you have all your

Podcasts library. In the app, you can manage your library, view top charts as well as search for trending Podcasts. The Apple TV app which has always been available on the iOS devices and the Apple TV is now available on your computer, offering you various movies and TV shows.

The Sidecar Feature

This feature allows you to use your iPad as a second screen for your Mac. Because you can use the Apple Pencil on your iPad, you can, in turn, use the iPad as a drawing tablet for apps like Photoshop when using on your computer. The Sidecar allows you to not only use the iPad as a second screen but also allows you to extend your display from your Mac to your iPad. You can access the feature from the System Preferences app on your computer, or place your mouse over the green button located on any app window of your computer or from the AirPlay interface on your computer. Later in the book, you would see an extensive guide on how to use this feature.

Find My

This app is also available in iOS 13 as well as iPadOS 13. It is a combination of the Find My Friends app and the Find My iPhone app. With this new app, you can track your devices even when the device is offline. To make this possible, Apple makes use of the devices of people who may be around the stolen or lost device as well as Bluetooth to securely send the location of your device to you. If you enabled Family sharing, you can also see all the devices belonging to your family members under your devices field in the app just like it was with the Find My iPhone app.

Screen Time

This is good news to lovers of this feature as the macOS Catalina has made it possible for the Mac to have the Screen time feature. This feature helps you to monitor how much time you spend using your devices which includes the iPad, iPhone, and Mac.

Safari

The Apple default browser is not left out of the improvements with the addition of the Siri Suggestions on your start page. The system makes use of the Siri Suggestions to display your iCloud tabs, bookmarks, reading list selections, frequently visited sites, as well as links that you received in your Message app to give you a more personal Safari start page. Safari has also included warnings for weak passwords when using a weak and easy to guess password on a new account. Apart from warning you that the password is weak, it also offers a better password to replace the one you indicated. The Safari app also has a new feature called the Picture-in-

Picture feature located at the tab audio button.

Mail App

The mail app in macOS Catalina now has a new feature to block emails from certain senders, unsubscribe from email lists and mute threads.

Revamped Reminders App

The reminders app experienced a total overhaul. This app now offers smart lists, new user interface, support for attaching documents to your reminders as well as integration with the Messages app to make it easy for you to create and manage your reminders. In chapter 5 of this user guide, I have extensively talked about how to maximize the full benefits of the new reminders app.

Chapter 1: Getting Started

How to Install macOS Catalina

- From your computer, go to the Dock and click on **System Preferences.**

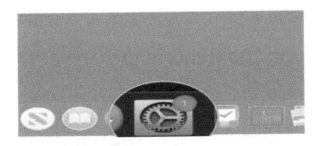

- **Tap Software Update** and your computer to check for any available software update.

- Tap **Upgrade Now.**

How to Backup Your iPad or iPhone on macOS Catalina

- Tap the **Finder** app located on your computer Dock.

- From the left side of your screen, under **Devices,** click on your device.

- Click on the **General** tab on your right.

- Go to the section for **Backup and Restore** and click on **Back Up Now.**

How to Restore Your iPad or iPhone on macOS Catalina

- Tap the **Finder** app located on your computer Dock.

- From the left side of your screen, under **Devices,** click on your device.

- Click on the **General** tab on your right.

- Go to the section for **Backup and Restore** and click on **Restore Backup**.

How to Turn on Automatic Updates

If you would want your computer to automatically download any new updates, you would have to enable automatic updates with the steps below:

- Navigate to the upper left side of your screen and click on the Apple icon.
- From the drop-down menu, click on **System Preferences**.
- Tap **Software Update**.

- Check the box beside
  "Automatically keep my Mac up
  to date."

How to Use Find My on macOS Catalina

The Find My app combines the Find My Friends and Find My iPhone apps and is available on iPadOS 13, macOS Catalina, iOS 13, and watchOS 6. The app comes installed as soon as you download the macOS Catalina. You would find it in the Application folder or your computer Dock. With the app, you can track both your friends and your devices.

How to Track Your Friends with Find My

- Launch the Find My app on your computer.
- Click on the **People** tab
- Navigate to the left of your screen and click on the person you want to track.
- You have 3 map views for a person; hybrid, default, and satellite.
- Use the + and – button to change the map size.

- Click on the location icon to tell your current location on the app map.
- If you want to share your current location with someone, click on **Share My Location**.
- Then input the name of the receiver in the To field.
- For persons not in your contact list, you can add them to the pop-up option.
- After you have added the person, click on **Send.**

How to Track Your Devices with Find My on Mac

All the devices registered under the Find My app are the ones that have your Apple ID and that of your family members.

- Launch the Find My app on your computer.

- Click on the **Devices** tab.

- Navigate to the left of your screen and click on the device you want to track.

- You have 3 map view for your device; hybrid, default, and satellite.

- Use the + and − button to change the map size.

- Click on the location icon to tell your current location on the app map.

How to Sign Documents on Mac Using your iPhone or iPad in Quick Look

- Click on the Finder icon on your computer to open the Finder window.

- Find the file you want to sign on and click once on the file.

- Tap your keyboard's space bar to view your document in **Quick Look.**

- Tap the **Markup** button.

- Click on the button for signature

- Tap the **iPhone or iPad**.

- Tap **Select Device**.

- Tap your personal iPad or iPhone from the device list.

- Endorse your signature on your iPad or iPhone.

- Click **Done** on the iPad or iPhone.

- The signature would appear in the signature menu on your computer. Click on it.

- Pull the signature to where you need it on the document.

- Click on **Done.**

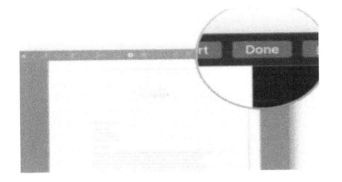

How to Sign Document on Mac in Preview

- Launch preview on your computer

- Open the desired document you want to append your signature.

- Tap **View.**

- Tap **Show Markup Toolbar.**

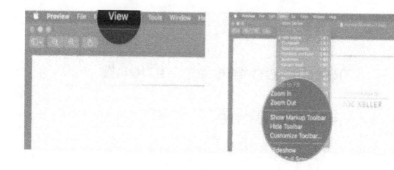

- Click on the signature button.

- Tap the **iPhone or iPad**.

- Choose **Select Device**.

- Tap your personal iPad or iPhone from the device list.

- Endorse your signature on your iPad or iPhone.

- Click **Done** on the iPad or iPhone.

- The signature would appear in the signature menu on your computer. Click on it.

- Pull the signature to where you need it on the document.

- Ensure to save your document.

How to Customize Apple Pencil Options

You have the option of customizing two settings for using the Apple pencil on Mac.

- From your computer, go to the Dock and click on **System Preferences**.

- Tap **Sidecar.**

- Set the field for **Enable double tap on Apple Pencil** to off or on with the checkbox.

- Set the field for **Show pointer when using Apple Pencil** to off or on with the checkbox.

Chapter 2: The Music app for Mac

How to Play Music in the Music App for Mac

- From the application folder or your computer Dock, launch the Music app.

- Hover your mouse over the playlist or album that you want to play and the play button would appear. Click on the play button.

- If your interest is to play a particular song, simply click on the playlist or album.

- Then tap the play button that would show on the track number or album art of the song when you hover over it in the track list.

How to Use Apple Music in the Music App

- From the application folder or your computer Dock, launch the Music app.

- Go to the sidebar and tap **For You** to view your Apple-curated suggestions and mixes, albums your friends have been listening to and recently played playlists and albums.

- From the sidebar, tap **Browse** to go through new music, trending artists, and other Apple Music available in the library.

- From the sidebar, tap **Radio** to access and play radio shows from Beats 1, both previously recorded and live shows.

- Navigate to the radio section and tap **Featured** to access Beats 1 streams highlighted by Apple, recently played radio content, and featured radio stations.

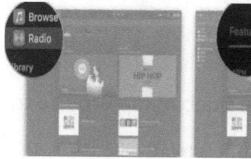

- From the Radio section, tap **Beats** 1 to access and play contents from **Beats** 1.

- Tap **Stations** in the same section to access available radio stations.

- If you want to add any album, song or playlist in the Music app to your library, use the + button.

How to View Your Music Library in the Music App

- From the application folder or your computer Dock, launch the Music app.
- Go to the sidebar and tap **Recently Added** for songs and

albums already in your library. This is not inclusive of playlists.

- From the sidebar, tap **Artists** to navigate through musical artists whose music is stored in your library.

  - In the menu bar, tap **View.**

  - Place your mouse over **Sort Albums By**.

  - Tap Rating, Year, Genre, or Title.

  - Select either **Descending** or **Ascending**.

 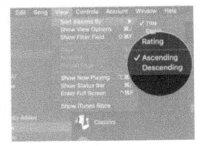

- From the sidebar, tap **Albums** to go through your music collections by the albums.

  - In the menu bar, tap **View.**

  - Then tap **Show View Options**.

  - Tap the drop-down beside **Sort by** and select either

Rating, Year, Artist, Genre, or Title.

- Tap the drop-down beside **Then** and select either Rating, Year, Artist, or Title.

- To view your songs, tap **Songs.**

  - Sort your song into categories by selecting either **Genre, Album, Artist, Time, Name** or other choice categories.

- go to the sidebar and click on a playlist to open it. You would notice that the playlists are arranged according to the origin.

The playlists created by iTunes come first then the ones subscribed to in Apple music or the ones created by you would follow in alphabetical order.

How to Import Music into the Music App

- From the application folder or your computer Dock, launch the Music app.
- Tap **File.**
- Tap **Import.**

- Select your choice file or folder to import.

- Tap **Open.**

How to Get Album and Song Info in the Music App

- From the application folder or your computer Dock, launch the Music app.

- You either right-click or control-click on an album or song.

- Then tap **Get Info.**

- To edit more than a single song, tap **Edit Items**.

- You can then edit information for **Details**, **Options**, **Artwork**, **Sorting**, **Lyrics**, and **File** tabs.

- Once done, tap **OK.**

How to Manage General Settings in the Music App

- From the application folder or your computer Dock, launch the Music app.

- Go to the menu bar and tap **Music.**

- Tap **Preferences.**

- From the General tab, tick the checkbox to enable **Always check for available downloads,**

Automatic Downloads, and **iCloud Music Library**,

- Tick the box beside **Show/ Hide** for Song list checkboxes, Star Ratings, and iTunes Store.

- Select list size in the next checkbox.

- Stop or allow notifications for song change by ticking the checkbox.

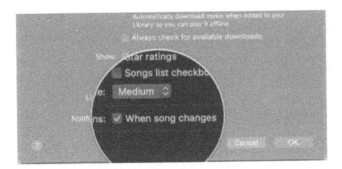

How to Manage Playback Settings in the Music App

- From the application folder or your computer Dock, launch the Music app.

- Go to the menu bar and tap **Music.**

- Tap **Preferences.**

- Tap **Playback.**

- Use the box beside **Crossfade Songs Playback** to activate crossfading.

- Drag the slider front and back to choose the length for the crossfade.

- Check the box for Sound Enhancer.

- Turn the Sound Enhancer high or low by moving the slider right or left.

- Enable **Sound Check** by ticking the box.

- Select the quality of your music video playback or downloads by clicking on the drop-down.

- If you want your followers to see your played music and also get music suggestions based on what you listen to on your computer, tick the box beside **Use Listening History.**

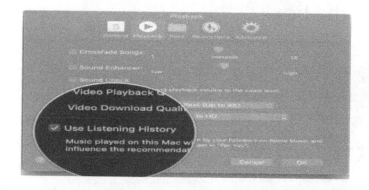

How to Manage Music File Settings

- From the application folder or your computer Dock, launch the Music app.

- Go to the menu bar and tap **Music.**

- Tap **Preferences.**

- Tap **Files.**

- Tap **Change** to change the media folder.

- Use the pop-up window to choose your preferred folder for storing music app media.

- Tap **Open.**

- Return to **Preferences,** then check the box beside **Keep Music Media folder organized** to have your music always organized in the library folder.

- Use the box for **Copy files to Music Media folder when adding to library** to decide if you want files dragged into the

library to be automatically added
to your media folder.

- Tap **Import Settings**.

- Use the next dropdown to
  determine the encoder format
  that imported music should
  come in, either **WAV, MP3, Apple
  Lossless, AIFF**, or **AAC**.

- Set the quality of the encoding by clicking on the next dropdown.

How to Set up Parental Controls

- From the application folder or your computer Dock, launch the Music app.
- Go to the menu bar and tap **Music.**
- Tap **Preferences.**

- Tap **Restrictions.**

- Tick the boxes beside Shared Libraries, Apple Music Profiles, Apple Music, and iTunes Store to disable or enable.

- In the next drop-down, select your desired country rating.

- To restrict music that has **explicit content,** check the box beside the option.

- The next drop-down allows you to select the maximum content rating allowed.

How to Reset Warnings in the Music App

- From the application folder or your computer Dock, launch the Music app.

- Go to the menu bar and tap **Music.**

- Tap **Preferences.**

- Tap **Advanced.**

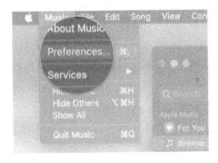 

- Tick the boxes beside "Automatically update artwork"

and "Add songs to Library when adding to playlists."

- Tap **Reset Warnings.**

- Tap **Reset Cache.**

- Tap the boxes beside **"Keep video playback on top of all other windows"** and **"Keep mini-player on top of all other windows."**

Chapter 3: How to Organize the Mac Desktop

How to Add Folders to Your Desktop

One fast way to organize your desktop is to add separate folders for separate purposes. The steps below would guide you on creating a folder:

- Ensure that the secondary click is activated, then right-click in an empty area on your computer's desktop.

- Then click on **New Folder.** Another shortcut is to use the

Command-Shift-N keys on your keyboard.

- Tap the title of the new folder.
- Then input your new name.
- Tap **Enter** on your keyboard.
- Drag items into the folder as desired.

How to Align and Sort Desktop Items Automatically

Sorting your items into a grid would give the placement of files and folders on your desktop some structure.

- Go to your desktop and right-click on any empty space.

- Tap **Clean Up By**.

- Select your preference, either kind, name, date created/ modified, tags or size.

How to Keep All your Desktop Files in a Grid Formation

The grid formation helps you to rearrange your scattered files and folders automatically. With this in place, every file you have on your desktop would always arrange into the grid except if you change the settings.

- Go to your desktop and right-click on any empty space.
- Tap **Sort By**.
- Tap **Snap to Grid**.

How to Change Grid Spacing on Desktop

- Go to your desktop and right-click on any empty space.
- Tap **Show View Options**.
- Use the slider to adjust the grid spacing to your preference.

How to Adjust the Size of Your Desktop Icons

If your icons appear too big or small, follow the steps below to modify the size.

- Go to your desktop and right-click on any empty space.
- Tap **Show View Options.**
- Use the slider to adjust the icon size to your preference.

How to Use macOS Stacks to Organize Your Desktop

This feature allows you to organize your desktop into files stacked according to categories and helps to keep your desktop organized as you add new files. Follow the steps below to enable Stacks:

- Go to the Finder menu bar and click on **View.**
- Choose **Use Stacks.** Another way to access this is to right-click on your desktop and select **Use Stacks**.

How to Turn Your iPad into a Second Screen with Sidecar

The sidecar is one great addition to the macOS Catalina. The feature allows you to spread your Mac display to your iPad. This would allow you to use the Apple pencil on your computer and perform tasks like sketching and drawing as well as mark up of PDFs and screenshots.

How to Setup Sidecar on Mac

Before you can use this feature, you have to first set it up on your iPad and computer.

- Go to the system dock and tap **System Preferences**.

- Tap **Sidecar.**

- Go to Connect to and click on **Devices.**

- Choose your iPad device from the dropdown on your screen.

- If you are unable to locate your iPad on the list, first connect it to your Mac and try again.

How to Setup Sidecar on iPad

The only thing you need to do to use sidecar on iPad is to ensure that both the mac and the iPad are connected to the same iCloud account. Both devices also need to be connected either through Bluetooth or directly.

How to Customize Sidecar on Mac

You have a variety of ways you can explore sidecar on your computer. Follow the steps below to customize

- From your computer, go to the Dock and click on **System Preferences**.
- Tap **Sidecar.**
- Besides the option for **Show Sidebar,** enable or disable the feature by ticking the box.

- If the **Show Sidebar** is enabled, use the switch to choose either right or left.

- Where applicable, tick the box to enable or disable **Show Touch Bar**.

- With **Show Touch Bar** enabled, use the switch to choose either top or bottom.

Chapter 4: The Notes App on Mac

How to Start a New Note

- Open the Notes app from Finder or Dock.

- Tap the button for **New note** (this is a pencil in a square icon). Another way is to go to the menu bar located on your screen top, click **File** then click **New Note.**

- Begin your note.

How to Make a Checklist

- Open the Notes app from Finder or Dock.
- Tap the button for **New note** (this is a pencil in a square icon). Another way is to go to the menu bar located on your screen top, click **File** then click **New Note**.
- Tap the button for checklist (icon showing a checkmark in a circle)
- Type your first content.

- On your keyboard, tap **Return** to instantly start a new checklist content.

How to Make a Numbered, Dashed or Bulleted List and Headings

- Open the Notes app from Finder or Dock.
- Tap the button for **New note** (this is a pencil in a square icon). Another way is to go to the menu bar located on your screen top, click **File** then click **New Note**.

- Go to the menu bar and tap **Format.**

- When you click on **Heading,** it would convert your next input into the heading.

- Choose from **Numbered List, Dashed List**, or **Bulleted List** depending on your desired list type.

- When ready to stop writing in a list, tap the **Return button** on a blank list item.

How to View Note Attachments

- Open the Notes app from Finder or Dock.

- From the toolbar, click the attachment button that looks like 4 squares.

- Then tap on the individual tabs like **Sketches, Photos & Videos,** and **Audio** to display the attachments.

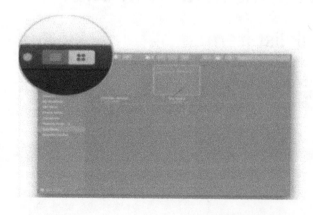

How to Set Password to Lock Notes

- Open the Notes app from Finder or Dock.

- Go to the menu bar at the screen top, click on **Notes** then click on **Preferences.**

- Tap **Set Password**.

- Type your new password.

- Again, repeat the password under **Verify.**

- You may choose to create a password hint.

- Tap **Set Password.**

How to Lock a Note

- Open the Notes app from Finder or Dock.
- Tap the Note you wish to lock.
- Tap the lock icon on the toolbar, a padlock-shape icon.

How to Sign in to iCloud

- From the Dock, open **System Preferences** or click the menu button at the left top side of your screen and select **System Preferences**.
- Tap **iCloud**.

- Input your iCloud details to log in.

- Check that the box beside **Notes** is ticked after you have signed in to iCloud under the menu option.

How to Invite Others to Collaborate on a Note

Before you can perform this function, other invitees need to have an iPad, iPhone or Mac.

- Open the Notes app from Finder or Dock.

- Tap the button to add people from the toolbar. This is a silhouette icon that has a + button.

- Select your preferred sharing method, that is, link, message, mail, etc.

- Input the phone number or email address of the invitees or

persons you want to share the
note with.

- Tap **Share.**

How to Send a Note to A Different App or Person

- Open the Notes app from Finder or Dock.
- Tap the note you wish to share.
- **Tap the share button** on the toolbar.
- Click on the app you want to share the note through.

How to Hide Apple Music on in the Music App for Mac

The steps below would show you how to hide the Apple Music app from view if you do not want to use it. You would then be left with just the playlists and library navigation in the sidecar.

- Launch the music app on your computer.
- Go to the menu bar and click on **Music.**
- Tap **Preferences.**
- Tap **Restrictions.**

- Go to the **Disable** section and tick the box beside **Apple Music.**

- Then tap **OK.** You would no longer see the section for Apple Music, Browse, For You and Radio on your sidebar and you would also not be able to access them.

Note: when the Apple music is disabled, you would still be able to access any Apple music albums and tracks that were previously added to your library along with any Apple Music playlists that you created or subscribed to.

How to Show the iTunes Store in the Music App on Mac

You would not see the iTunes Music Store on the music app on macOS Catalina without first enabling the feature. Even after you have discontinued your subscription or hidden the Apple music, you can still receive new music from the iTunes store. Follow the steps below to first show the iTunes store.

- Launch the music app on your computer.
- Tap **View.**

- Select **Preferences.**

- Navigate to **General** and tick the box beside **iTunes Store.**

- Tap **OK.** You would now see the iTunes store on the sidebar.

Chapter 5: How to Use Reminders on Mac

The reminders app helps you keep track of important tasks, create a shopping list and perform other functions. You can make use of iCloud or other third-party services to sync your to-dos across your iPad, iPhone, and Mac.

How to Add a Reminders Account Provider

- From Dock, open **Reminders.**

- Go to the menu bar and tap **Reminders.**

- Click on **Add Account.**

- Select the type of Reminders account of your choice, e.g. Exchange.

- Tap **Continue.**

- Input your account credentials.

- Tap **Sign In.**

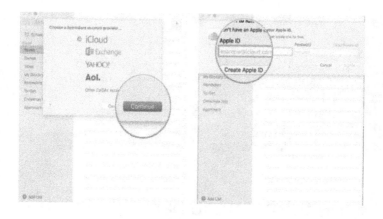

- Tick the box beside **Reminders** if it is not ticked already, then select the apps you want to use your account with.

- Tap **Add Account**.

How to Create a Reminder

- From Dock, open **Reminders.**

- Tap the + button.

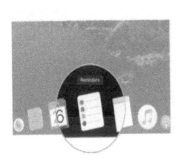 

- Type out the contents of your reminder.

How to Schedule a Due Date for Reminder

- From Dock, open **Reminders.**

- Hover your cursor over the reminder and an info button would appear (an "I" icon), click on this button.
- Check the box next to **On a Day**.
- Select the reminder date and time.
- Tap **Done**.

How to Schedule a Due Date for Reminder

In macOS Catalina, the steps to add a due date is different from other software.

- From the application folder or your Dock, open **Reminders.**

- Tap the text for the reminder you wish to add the date.

- Tap the button for **Add Date**.

- You can tap any of the suggestions if they apply or pick your own date.

- Tap **Add Time**.

- You can tap any of the suggestions if they apply or pick your own time.

How to Set Up a Location Notification for a Reminder

- From the application folder or your Dock, open **Reminders.**
- Hover your cursor over the reminder and an info button would appear (an "I" icon), click on this button.
- Tick the box beside **At a Location**.
- Enter the location of your choice.
- Click on either **Leaving** or **Arriving**.
- From the map, drag the dot farther or closes from the pin to

the area where the reminder
should take place.

- Click on **Done.**

How to Add Location in macOS Catalina

- From the application folder or your Dock, open **Reminders.**
- Go to the reminder you want to add the location and click on the text.
- Tap the button for **Add Location.**
- You can tap any of the suggestions if they apply or

manually type your preferred location.

- Click on the suggestion that appears from the list.

How to Create a New List

- From the application folder or your Dock, open **Reminders.**
- Tap **Add List**.
- Input your desired name for the list.

How to Rename a List

- From the application folder or your Dock, open **Reminders.**

- Go to the list you want to rename and right-click on it.

- Select **Rename.**

- Enter the new name for the list.

How to Delete a List

- From the application folder or your Dock, open **Reminders.**

- Go to the list you want to delete and right-click on it.

- Select **Delete.**

How to Move a Reminder to Another List

- From the application folder or your Dock, open **Reminders.**
- Tap the list that contains the reminder you want to move.
- Click and hold down on the reminder you want to change the location for.
- Then drag the reminder to the new list.

How to Share a List with Another iCloud User

- From the application folder or your Dock, open **Reminders.**
- Hover your cursor over the list name and a share button would appear, click on this button.
- Select the contact to share the list with.
- Tap **Done.**

How to Share Reminder List in macOS Catalina

- From the application folder or your Dock, open **Reminders.**

- Hover your cursor over the list name and a share button would appear, click on this button.

- Click on your preferred sharing method, e.g. AirDrop or Mail.

- If you selected **Messages or Mail**, tap **Share.**

- Enter the email address, name or phone number of the receiver.

- Tap **Send.**

- if you choose **AirDrop** or **Copy Link,** enter the email address, name or phone number of the receiver.

- Tap **Share.**

How to Group Reminder Lists in macOS Catalina

- From the application folder or your Dock, open **Reminders.**

- Drag one list on the top of another list.

- Set a name for the group.

How to Add a Message Notification for a Reminder

This new software upgrade allows you to set a reminder to notify you when next you message a specified contact.

- From the application folder or your Dock, open **Reminders.**
- Hover your cursor over the reminder you want to add the Messages reminder to and an info button would appear (an "i" icon), click on this button.

- tick the box beside **When Messaging a Person.**

- Click on **Contact Name**.

- type the name of the contact or scroll through the list to locate the contact.

- Select the name of the preferred contact.

How to Add Attachments to a Reminder

- From the application folder or your Dock, open **Reminders.**
- Hover your cursor over the reminder you want to add the Messages reminder to and an info button would appear (an "i" icon), click on this button.

- Click on **Add Image.**

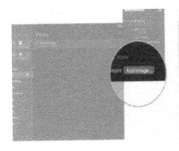 

- Tap **Photos** and browse through your Photo Library to select and add photos.

- If you wish to create your own images or import images from an iOS device, click the button for **Add Sketch, Scan Documents**, or **Take Photo.**

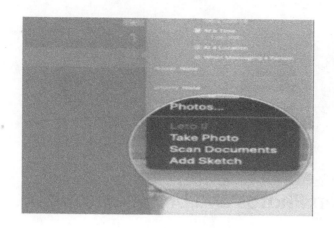

Chapter 6: The Podcasts App on your Mac

macOS Catalina broke the iTunes into different dedicated apps which made it possible for the computer to have its own Podcasts app. The app allows you to subscribe to, manage your podcast library and also search for podcasts. This is similar to the Podcasts app on your iOS device. In this chapter, you would learn all there is to know about the podcasts app.

How to Play a Podcast in the Podcasts App

- From the application folder, Launchpad or your Dock, open the **Podcasts app.**

- To listen to any podcast, click on the podcast photo for that podcast.

- Irrespective of the tab you are in, whether searching for new broadcast or you want to continue the last podcast you started, whenever you click on a podcast, the app would automatically play the podcast for you.

How to Search for a Podcast in the App

- From the application folder, Launchpad or your Dock, open the **Podcasts app.**
- Click on the search bar located in the sidebar.

- Enter your search phrase.

- On your keyboard, click on **Return/Enter.**

- All the options that fit your search term would be displayed for shows and episodes.

How to Find a Podcast in Your Podcast Library

Follow the steps below to find an episode from a podcast or a podcast itself in the app library.

- From the application folder, Launchpad or your Dock, open the **Podcasts app.**

- Click on the search bar located in the sidebar.

- Click on the tab for **Your Library**.

- Input your search phrase.

- On your keyboard, click on **Return/Enter**

How to Subscribe to a Podcast in the App

When you subscribe to a podcast, it automatically gets added to your library which means that each time new episodes are available, you would be able to see and listen to them.

- From the application folder, Launchpad or your Dock, open the **Podcasts app.**
- Search for the desired podcast.
- Hover your mouse on the podcast photo until you see the button for play and options appear on your screen.
- Click on **Options.** It is a three dots icon.
- Tap **Subscribe.**

How to Unsubscribe to a Podcast

You can always unsubscribe to a particular podcast but note that this will not delete the existing podcasts from your library, you would just not receive new episodes added to your library.

- From the application folder, Launchpad or your Dock, open the **Podcasts app.**
- Search for the desired podcast.
- Hover your mouse on the podcast photo until you see the

button for play and options appear on your screen.

- Click on **Options.** It is a three dots icon.

- Tap **Unsubscribe.**

How to Delete a Podcast from Your Podcasts App

The steps below would guide you on how to delete a podcast from your library.

- From the application folder, Launchpad or your Dock, open the **Podcasts app.**
- Search for the desired podcast in your library.
- Hover your mouse on the podcast photo until you see the button for play and options appear on your screen.

- Click on **Options.** It is a three dots icon.

- Tap **Delete from library**

How to Play a Podcast Next in Queue in the App

- From the application folder, Launchpad or your Dock, open the **Podcasts app.**

- Search for the desired podcast to play next to your app library.

- Hover your mouse on the podcast photo until you see the button for play and options appear on your screen.

- Click on **Options.** It is a three dots icon.

- Tap **Play Next.**

How to View the Top Charts in the Podcasts App

The podcasts app presents you with the hot and trending content in the podcast world. Follow the steps below to view this.

- From the application folder, Launchpad or your Dock, open the **Podcasts app.**
- Go to the sidebar and click on **Top Charts.**

- On the next page, you would see the top episode and shows of podcasts that other Podcasts users are listening to.

How to Share a Podcast in the App

You can share podcasts to friends using different methods like messages, AirDrop, email, Notes with the steps highlighted below:

- From the application folder, Launchpad or your Dock, open the **Podcasts app.**

- Search for the podcast you wish to share.

- Hover your mouse on the podcast photo until you see the button for play and options appear on your screen.

- Click on **Options.** It is a three dots icon.

- Tap **Share Show or Share Episode**.

- Select your preferred sharing
  method.
- Depending on your preferred
  method, follow the instructions
  on the screen to input additional
  information. Each method has its
  own requirements.

How to Change the Order Episodes Get Played in the App

- From the application folder, Launchpad or your Dock, open the **Podcasts app.**
- Search for the podcast which you would not want to receive notifications for.
- Hover your mouse on the podcast photo until you see the button for play and options appear on your screen.

- Click on **Options.** It is a three

  dots icon.

- Tap **Settings.**

- Select your preferred option

  from the displayed list. The

  options include

  - Play Most Recent First

  - Play in Sequential Order

  - Custom Settings

  - Only Keep the Most Recent

    Episodes

Chapter 7: Sync Your iPad and iPhone with Your Computer

With the absence of iTunes, you may be wondering how you can sync your iPad and iPhones with your computer. There is no need to worry as this chapter would cover all you need to know about syncing your devices on your computer.

How to Sync on macOS Catalina

In the absence of the iTunes, you can make use of Finder to sync your iPad and iPhone with the steps below

- Tap the **Finder** app located on your computer Dock.

- From the left side of your screen, under **Devices,** click on your device.
- On the next screen, you would find a similar interface from macOS Mojave.
- In this screen, you can manage backups, restore your device and sync content from your mobile devices to your computer and back as well as transfer files between devices on this screen.

How to Sync Music to Your Mobile Devices on macOS Catalina

Note: you would be unable to sync music through your computer if you are using the iCloud music library sync on your mobile devices.

- Tap the **Finder** app located on your computer Dock.
- From the left side of your screen, under **Devices,** click on your device.
- Click on the music tab on your right.

- Activate music syncing by checking the box for **"Sync Music onto your device"**.
- Under the option for sync, you have two options to choose from: **"Selected playlists, artists, albums, and genres"** or "Entire music library".
- From the section for **Options,** you can select to include the 3 available options which are:
  - ➤ **automatically fill free space with songs**
  - ➤ **voice memos**
  - ➤ **include videos**

- where applicable, select artists, playlists, genre, and albums.

- Tap **Apply.**

- Once done, tap **Sync** so that your music file would sync between your mobile device and computer.

How to Sync Movies Between Your Mobile Devices on macOS Catalina

- Tap the **Finder** app located on your computer Dock.

- From the left side of your screen, under **Devices,** click on your device.

- Click on the movies tab on your right.

- Activate movie syncing by checking the box for **"Sync Movies onto your device"**.

- Go to Sync and click the box for **Automatically include.**

- Use the pull-down option to choose all content or select your preference from the listed options.

- Tap **Apply.**

- Tap **Sync** to have the movies sync between your mobile device and the computer.

How to Sync TV Shows to Your iPad or iPhone

- Tap the **Finder** app located on your computer Dock.

- From the left side of your screen, under **Devices,** click on your device.

- Click on the TV tab on your right.

- Activate TV show syncing by checking the box for **"Sync TV Shows onto your device"**

- Go to Sync and click the box for **Automatically include.**

- Use the pull-down option to choose **all unwatched** or select your preference from the listed options.

- In the pull-down menu following, select either **selected shows** or **all shows.**

- If you went for selected shows, check the boxes beside the shows that you want to be synced.

- Tap **Apply.**

- Tap **Sync** to have the TV shows sync between your mobile device and the computer.

How to Sync Podcasts to Your iPad or iPhone

- Tap the **Finder** app located on your computer Dock.

- From the left side of your screen, under **Devices,** click on your device.

- Click on the **Podcast** tab on your right.

- Activate podcast syncing by checking the box for **"Sync Podcast onto your device".**

- Go to Sync and click the box for **Automatically Copy**.

- Use the pull-down option to choose **all unplayed** or select your preference from the listed options.
- In the pull-down menu following, select either **selected shows** or **all podcasts.**
- If you went for selected podcasts, check the boxes beside the podcasts that you want to be synced.
- Tap **Apply.**
- Tap **Sync** to have the podcasts sync between your mobile device and the computer.

How to Sync Audiobooks to Your iPad or iPhone

- Tap the **Finder** app located on your computer Dock.

- From the left side of your screen, under **Devices,** click on your device.

- Click on the **Audiobook** tab on your right.

- Activate audiobook syncing by checking the box for **"Sync Audiobook onto your device"**.

- In the pull-down menu following, select either **selected audiobooks** or **all audiobooks.**

- If you went for selected audiobooks, check the boxes beside the audiobooks that you want to be synced.

- Tap **Apply.**

- Tap **Sync** to have the audiobooks sync between your mobile device and the computer.

How to Sync Book to Your iPad or iPhone

- Tap the **Finder** app located on your computer Dock.

- From the left side of your screen, under **Devices,** click on your device.

- Click on the **Book** tab on your right.

- Activate book syncing by checking the box for **"Sync Book onto your device"**.

- In the pull-down menu following, select either **Selected Books** or **All Books.**

- If you went for selected books, check the boxes beside the books that you want to be synced.

- Tap **Apply.**

- Tap **Sync** to have the books sync between your mobile device and the computer.

How to Sync Photos to Your iPad or iPhone

- Tap the **Finder** app located on your computer Dock.

- From the left side of your screen, under **Devices,** click on your device.

- Click on the **Photos** tab on your right.

- Activate book syncing by checking the box for **"Sync Photos onto your device".**

- In the pull-down menu following, select either **Selected Photos** or **All Photos.**

- If you went for selected Photos, check the boxes beside the Photos that you want to be synced.

- Tap **Apply.**

- Tap **Sync** to have the Photos sync between your mobile device and the computer.

How to Sync Files to Your iPad or iPhone

- Tap the **Finder** app located on your computer Dock.

- From the left side of your screen, under **Devices,** click on your device.

- Click on the **Files** tab on your right.

- Activate book syncing by checking the box for **"Sync Files onto your device".**

- In the pull-down menu following, select either **Selected Files** or **All Files.**

- If you went for selected files, check the boxes beside the files that you want to be synced.

- Tap **Apply.**

- Tap **Sync** to have the files sync between your mobile device and the computer.

Chapter 8: Apple TV App for Mac

The Apple TV app which has always been available on iOS devices got added to the Mac, all thanks to macOS Catalina. You can now continue your current movies and shows across your computer, iPad or iPhone without having to start all over again. The major difference between the TV app on your Mac and that on other platforms is the apps itself. The TV app on your mobile devices works with other third-party apps like NBC to bring together all your favorite content in one single location. This option is not available on the TV app for Mac.

How to Watch a Movie or Show in the TV App

- Launch the TV app from the application folder or your Dock.
- Click on a movie or show from **Up Next** to begin watching it instantly.
- Otherwise, navigate to **What to Watch** or other movie and TV sections.
- Click on the movie or show of your choice.

- Tap **Play.**

How to Watch Apple TV+ Shows in the App

The Apple TV+ went live on November 1, 2019 and offers varieties of unique content by Apple.

- Launch the Apple TV on your computer.
- Use your two fingers to scroll or swipe on the Apple TV+ section.

You would see this under **What to Watch.**

- Tap the show you want to view
- Tap **Play Episode** or **Play.**

How to Add Movies and Shows to Up Next

Whenever you need something entertaining to watch, your first stop should be the Up Next.

- Launch the TV app on your computer.
- Play any TV show or movie of your choice in the app to have

the content automatically added to **Up Next.**

- Otherwise, tap any piece of content in any of the sections under **Up Next.**

- Then tap **Add to Up Next.**

How to Play Videos from Your Library in the TV App

With this new update, you no longer have to go to different apps for TV shows and movies to watch content that you purchased on your Apple TV as all can be viewed in this ap.

- Launch the TV app on your computer.
- Navigate to the screen top and tap **Library.**
- Select any of the following options from the sidebar:

> **Genres:** choose one of the available genres.

> **Downloaded:** Shows or Movies that you downloaded to your computer to view when offline.

➢ **TV Shows:** Your collection of purchased TV shows.

➢ **Movies:** Your collection of purchased movies.

➢ **Recently Added:** Movies and TV shows recently added to your personal content library.

- Tap the show or movie you want to watch.

- Hover on your chosen episode or movie until you see the play button. Click on the button and your content would download and play.

How to Buy TV Shows and Movies in the App

- Launch the TV app on your computer.
- Navigate to the screen top and tap **TV Shows** or **Movies.**
- Tap the title you want to rent or buy.
- Tap **Rent** or **Buy,** whichever is available.

- Otherwise, use the search bar.

- Input the name of your desired content.

- Select the title from the results on your screen.

- Tap **Rent** or **Buy,** whichever is available.

How to Subscribe to Channels in the TV App

You can subscribe to any desired channels that are available like the Cinemax just like you do on your Apple TV, iPad or iPhone.

- Launch the TV app.

- Go to **Apple TV Channels** and tap the desired channel.

- Click **Try It Free.**

- Input your password.

- Tap **Buy.**

- Then tap **Confirm.**

Note: once the free trial is over, you would then get charged for subsequent subscription service.

How to Cancel Channel Subscription on Your Computer

- From your Application folder or Dock, click on **System Preferences.**

- Tap **Apple ID**.

- Select **Media & Purchases**

- Then click on **Manage** beside **Subscriptions**.

- Tap **Edit** beside **channel subscription** o your active subscription list. If this is to cancel while the free trial is on, you would see the option close to the bottom.

- Tap **Cancel Subscription**.

- Then click on **Confirm**.

How to Manage Downloads in the TV App

- Launch the TV app.
- Go to the menu bar and click **TV.**
- Tap **Preferences.**
- Go to the **General** panel and tick the box beside **Always check for available downloads** if you would like the app to always check for available downloads.
- Select both or either the boxes for TV Shows and boxes to automatically download both or download either TV episodes or movies.

- Check the box beside **"Checkboxes in Library."** This option means that only the contents that you check in your library would sync automatically.

- Click the drop-down beside **List Size** to choose a new size.

How to Manage Settings for Video Playback in the TV App

- Launch the TV app.
- Go to the menu bar and click **TV.**
- Tap **Preferences.**
- Tap **Playback.**

- Set the streaming media quality using the drop-down menu beside **Streaming Quality**.
- Set the streaming media quality using the drop-down menu beside **Download Quality**.
- If you want the TV app to download HDR and multichannel audio where available, tick the appropriate boxes.
- If you want the app to use your viewing history to present recommendations to you, tick the box for the Viewing history.

How to Manage Media Files in the TV App

- Launch the TV app.

- Go to the menu bar and click **TV.**

- Tap **Preferences.**

- Tap **Files.**

- To change the location for storing media, click on **Change.** To reset to the default storage location, click on **Reset.**

- Choose another folder for storing media on the app using the pop-up window.
- Tap **Open.**
- Go back to Preference, (un)check the option for **Keep Media folder organized** if you want to have your media organized in the folder you chose for your media.
- (Un)check the option for "**Copy files to Media folder when adding to library**" if you want the files you drag into your

library to be automatically added to the media folder.

- You may (un)check the last box to set the TV shows and movies to be automatically deleted as soon as you are done viewing them.

How to Set up Parental Controls

- Launch the TV app.
- Go to the menu bar and click **TV.**
- Tap **Preferences.**
- Tap **Restrictions.**
- Tap the checkboxes to enable or disable the iTunes Store for TV

show and movie purchases as well as shared libraries.

- Choose your preferred country rating by using the next drop-down.

- Tick the box to restrict TV shows and Movies to specified ratings.

- Select the rating maturity limit for TV shows and movies by using the drop-down option.

How to Reset Cache and Warnings and Also Clear Play History

- Launch the TV app.
- Go to the menu bar and click **TV.**

- Tap **Preferences.**

- Tap **Advanced.**

- Tap **Reset Warnings**.

- Then tap **Reset Cache**.

- Tap **Clear Play History**.

Chapter 9: How to Use Screen Time on Mac

The macOS Catalina introduced the Screen Time feature on Macs for the first time. This feature has been available on iPads and iPhones since 2018 and it helps to control the amount of time that you spend on several apps including games and social media. It also helps to limit your usage to these apps. We would discuss how to use this feature in the guide below.

How to Turn on Screen Time on macOS

You would find the screen time in System Preferences on your computer. Follow the steps below to turn it on

- From System Preferences, click on **Screen Time.**

- At the bottom left of your screen, click on the **Options** button.
- Go to the top right of your screen and click on **Turn On**.
- Screen time is ready for use.

How to Turn Off Screen Time

Follow the steps below to turn off screen time on your computer

- From System Preferences, click on **Screen Time**.
- At the bottom left of your screen, click on the **Options** button.

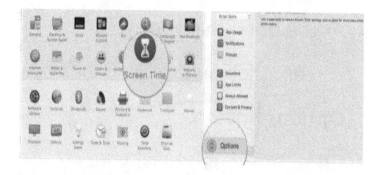

- Go to the top right of your screen and click on **Turn Off.**

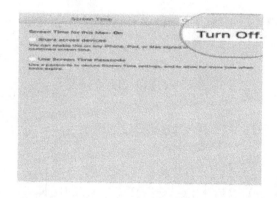

How to Share Screen Time Across All Devices

When you share the Screen Time across all your devices, it helps to give you a truer picture of the amount of time you spend on apps and activities. Follow the steps below to activate this

- From System Preferences, click on **Screen Time.**
- At the bottom left of your screen, click on the **Options** button.

- Navigate to the option for **Share Across Devices** and tick the box.

How to Add a Password to Screen Time on macOS

- From System Preferences, click on **Screen Time**.
- At the bottom left of your screen, click on the **Options** button.

- Navigate to the option for **Use Screen Time Password** and tick the box.

How to View App Usage in Screen Time on macOS

- From System Preferences, click on **Screen Time.**
- On the left side of your screen, click on the **App Usage** button.

- The next screen would show you your app usage by categories, apps and by the day. You would also be able to see apps that have limits on this screen.

How to Access Sent Notifications in Screen Time on macOS

The steps below would guide you on how to see who sent what notifications on your Mac.

- From System Preferences, click on **Screen Time**.

- On the left side of your screen, click on the **Notifications** button.

- The next screen would display all your notifications by week, day or sender.

How to View Pickups in Screen Time

If you have shared the Screen Time across all your devices, you can view the number of times you picked up your mobile devices from your computer.

- From System Preferences, click on **Screen Time**.

- On the left side of your screen, click on the **Pickups** button.

How to Schedule Downtime Using Screen Time on macOS

When Downtime is active, the only apps that can work are the ones that you gave permissions to. Follow the steps below to schedule downtime on your computer.

- From System Preferences, click on **Screen Time**.

- On the left side of your screen, click on the **Downtime** button.

- Click on **Turn On** to enable Downtime.

- Select your schedule using the radio buttons, choose either **Custom** or **Every Day** as desired.

- If you selected **Every Day,** downtime would happen at the same time every day. If Custom is selected, you can choose downtime to happen at different times each day or choose for it not to happen on a particular day in a week.

How to Set Limits Using Screen Time

- From System Preferences, click on **Screen Time**.
- On the left side of your screen, click on the **App Limits** button.
- Click on **Turn On** to enable App Limits.
- Use the + button to add an app category.
- Then tick the box beside the app category you want to limit.
- Once the app category is highlighted, use the radio buttons to set your limit, choose either **Custom** or **Every Day.**

- Repeat steps 5 and 6 for all the apps category you want to limit.

- Tap **Done** to finish up.

How to Remove App Limits

- From System Preferences, click on **Screen Time**.

- On the left side of your screen, click on the **App Limits** button.

- On the right, untick the boxes beside each app category you no longer want the limit on.

- Click on **Turn Off** to disable App tracking.

How to Set Always Allowed Content in Screen Time

There are times when you would need some certain processes to work regardless of the restrictions that exist. Follow the guide below to set this feature

- From System Preferences, click on **Screen Time.**

- On the left side of your screen, click on the **Always Allowed** button.

- Check the box beside all the items you want to always allow.

How to Set Content and Privacy for Screen Time on macOS

The steps below would guide you on how to restrict privacy and content on your computer using the Screen Time feature.

- From System Preferences, click on **Screen Time**.
- On the left side of your screen, click on the **Content & Privacy** button.
- Click on **Turn On** to enable Content & Privacy.

- On the next screen, you would be presented with 4 sections; Content, Apps, Stores, and Other.

- Check the box under each section to complete.

Chapter 10: How to Use Voice Controls on Mac

The new software allows you to control your computer with your speech. This feature is more beneficial to persons with limited mobility, dexterity and other conditions. Apart from persons in this category, you can also make use of this feature to interact with your devices across the iPad, iPhone, and Mac.

How to Activate Voice Control on Mac

If this is your first time to use this feature on your computer, you would need to first set it up with the steps below:

- From your computer, go to the Dock and click on **System Preferences**.
- Tap **Accessibility**.
- From this page, click on **Voice Control** under the section for **Motor**.

- Go to **"Enable Voice Control"** and tick the box.

How to Wake or Sleep Voice Control on Mac

The steps below would guide you on how to wake as well as sleep the Voice Control feature

- From the Voice Control icon, click on **Wake** to wake the feature.
- From the Voice Control icon, click on **Sleep** to wake the feature. When this mode is

active, the Voice Control feature would not work.

How to Change the Voice Control Language on Mac

When setting up Voice Control, it uses your default system language. However, you can change the language with the steps below:

- From your computer, go to the Dock and click on **System Preferences**.
- Tap **Accessibility**.

- From this page, click on **Voice Control** under the section for **Motor.**

- Navigate to **Language** and tap the pull-down menu.

- Click on **Customize.**

- Click the box beside the language(s) you want to add.

- Tap **OK.**

How to Select a New Language in Voice Control on Mac

- Click on the existing language on the Voice control icon located at the right part of your computer.

- Then select the new language you want to use.

How to Disable/Enable Commands in Voice Control on Mac

You are able to disable or enable any Voice Control command both the ones you created yourself and the ones created by Apple.

- From your computer, go to the Dock and click on **System Preferences**.
- Tap **Accessibility**.

- From this page, click on **Voice Control** under the section for **Motor.**
- Tap the button for **Commands.**
- To disable, uncheck the boxes beside the desired commands.
- To enable, check the boxes beside the desired commands.
- Tap **Done.**

How to Create Custom Commands in Voice Control on Mac

The steps below would teach you how to add personal commands on your computer:

- From your computer, go to the Dock and click on **System Preferences.**

- Tap **Accessibility.**

- From this page, click on **Voice Control** under the section for **Motor.**

- Tap the button for **Commands.**

- Choose +

- Then go to space for **"When I say"** and add your command. By default, whatever command you input would apply to all your apps.

- If you want the app to apply to just one app, tap the pull-down menu beside **"While Using."**
- Then select the app that should work with the command.
- Click on the drop-down menu beside **"Performed"** and select how the command should perform.
- Tap **Done.**

How to Delete Custom Commands in Voice Control

Follow the guide below to permanently delete any Voice controls custom command.

- From your computer, go to the Dock and click on **System Preferences**.
- Tap **Accessibility**.
- From this page, click on **Voice Control** under the section for **Motor.**
- Tap the button for **Commands.**

- Go to Custom and select the command you want to delete.
- Then tap the – button.
- Tap **Delete** to approve your action.

How to Change the Microphone for Voice Control on Mac

The Voice Control feature uses the built-in microphone on your computer by default. But you can change to another available microphone.

- From your computer, go to the Dock and click on **System Preferences**.

- Tap **Accessibility**.

- From this page, click on **Voice Control** under the section for **Motor**.

- Tap the Pull-down menu beside **Microphone**.

- Then select the microphone of your choice from the list.

How to Receive an Alert When Voice Control Recognizes a Command

You can set up this feature to alert you whenever it recognizes a sound. Follow the steps below:

- From your computer, go to the Dock and click on **System Preferences**.
- Tap **Accessibility**.
- From this page, click on **Voice Control** under the section for **Motor**.

- Check the box beside **"Play sound when command is recognized."**

Chapter 11: Safari on macOS Catalina

In this section of the book, we would talk about how to use the Safari browser on your Mac.

How to Visit a Website

- Use the Finder or Dock to launch the Safari Browser.
- Then click on the address bar. You would see this at the top of your window.
- Input the website address.
- Tap **Return** on your keyboard.

How to Search with the Address Bar

You can use the address bar to input the website address as well as to search on Google.

- Use the Finder or Dock to launch the Safari Browser.
- Then click on the address bar. You would see this at the top of your window.
- Enter your search terms e.g. iPhone 11 release date
- Tap **Return** on your keyboard.
- Safari would display the search results from Google.

How to Bookmark a Website

When you bookmark a website, it helps you to easily return to that website by clicking on the bookmark link. Follow the steps below to bookmark.

- Use the Finder or Dock to launch the Safari Browser.
- Then click on the address bar. You would see this at the top of your window.
- Input the website address.
- Tap **Return** on your keyboard.

- Once the website opens, click **Command-D** on your keyboard.

- Put your preferred title for the bookmark or use the existing title. Input description if desired.

- Tap **Return** on your keyboard or click **Add.**

- Go to the menu bar and click on **View.** You would see this at the top left of your screen.

- Then click on **Show Favorites Bar.**

- You would see all your bookmarked pages below the

address bar. To access any, simply click on it.

How to View All Your Bookmarks

The steps below would guide you on how to view all your bookmarks at once.

- Use the Finder or Dock to launch the Safari Browser.
- Tap the **Show sidebar** option beside your address bar.
- Then click on the **Bookmarks tab** if it is currently not there. It has an icon like an open book.

How to Remove Bookmarks

You can always remove any bookmark with the steps below

- Use the Finder or Dock to launch the Safari Browser.
- Go to the menu bar and click on **Bookmarks.** You would see this at the top left of your screen.
- Then click on **Edit Bookmarks.**
- Tap the arrow beside **Favorites.**
- Then control-click or Right-click on the bookmark you want to delete.
- Click on **Delete.**

How to Add a Web Page to Your Reading List

Pages that you add to your reading list would be available for you to read them later. It is important to note that you would not need an internet connection to read pages added to the reading list.

- Use the Finder or Dock to launch the Safari Browser.
- Navigate to the website you want to add to the reading list.

- Click on **command-shift-D** on your keyboard to add that page to the reading list.

How to View Your Reading List

- Use the Finder or Dock to launch the Safari Browser.
- Tap the **Show sidebar** option beside your address bar.
- Then click on the **reading list tab**. It has an icon like a pair of glasses.
- Click on the item you want to read.

How to Delete Items from your Reading List

If you no longer need a page to show under your reading list, follow the steps below to delete the page:

- Use the Finder or Dock to launch the Safari Browser.
- Tap the **Show sidebar** option beside your address bar.
- Then click on the **reading list tab**. It has an icon like a pair of glasses.

- Next, control-click or right-click on the page that you want to delete from the list.

- Then click on **Remove Item**.

How to Enable Private Browsing

When you surf the internet on Private browsing, your search history, websites visited as well as your AutoFill information would not be saved. It gives you some required privacy.

- Use the Finder or Dock to launch the Safari Browser.

- Go to the menu bar and click on **File.** You would see this at the top left of your screen.

- Then click on **New Private Window.**

- Another way to do this is to press **command-shift-N** on your keyboard.

How to Add Extensions to Safari

These extensions when added to the browser give new functions to Safari. They are used to integrate with apps, block ads, and several other functions. We have several free extensions that are useful in terms of productivity, provides entertainment, security and lots more.

- Use the Finder or Dock to launch the Safari Browser.

- Go to the menu bar and click on **Safari.** You would see this at the top left of your screen.

- Then click on **Safari Extensions**.

- You would be taken to the Safari Extensions page on the Mac App Store to download and install extensions of your choice, just like you would download and install other apps.

- Once the installation is done, launch the app to get it added to the browser toolbar.

How to Pin Tabs

If you have sites that you visit very often, you can Pin them to be able to easily access them in the future.

- Use the Finder or Dock to launch the Safari Browser.
- Go to the menu bar and click on **View.** You would see this at the top left of your screen.
- Then click on **Show Tab Bar.**

- Navigate to the web page you want to pin.

- Click and hold down on the desired tab.

- Then drag it to the left side of your computer.

- You would see the first letter of the website or a little site logo on the left part of the tab bar.

- To remove pages from the pinned tab, simply pull them to the right.

How to Set the Homepage

The homepage on your Safari, by default, is apple.com. however, the steps below would guide you on changing the default homepage.

- Use the Finder or Dock to launch the Safari Browser.
- Go to the menu bar and click on **Safari.** You would see this at the top left of your screen.
- Then click on the **General tab**.
- Input your desired website beside the **Homepage.**

- Alternatively, navigate to the website and then click on **Set to Current Page** to set that page as your default.
- Navigate to "**New windows open with**" and tap the dropdown menu.
- Then tap the **Homepage** for every new window you open to launch the homepage.
- Navigate to "**New tabs open with**" and tap the dropdown menu.

- Then tap the **Homepage** for every new tab you open to launch the homepage.

How to Share Websites

The steps below would guide you on how to share a website.

- Use the Finder or Dock to launch the Safari Browser.
- Navigate to the website you want to share.
- From the top right side of your browser, click on **Share Sheet.**
- Select a sharing method. Options include email, Reminders, Notes,

AirDrop, Messages, and other third-party supported apps.

How to Use Reader View

This view strips a page of all the fancy animations or movements leaving you with just the words and images. While not all the websites support this feature, a variety of websites support it.

- Go to a website and click on the button for **Reader View**. You would see this at the left of the address bar.

How to Modify Font in Reader View

- Go to a website and click on the button for **Reader View**. you would see this on the left side of the address bar.
- Then click on the button for **Reader Options.** This is the two As icon located at the right of the address bar.
- Then tap your preferred font.

How to Adjust Background Color in Reader View

- Go to a website and click on the button for **Reader View.** you would see this on the left side of the address bar.

- Then click on the button for **Reader Options**. This is the two As icon located at the right of the address bar.

- Then tap your preferred background color.

How to Modify Font Size in Reader View

- Go to a website and click on the button for **Reader View**. you would see this on the left side of the address bar.

- Then click on the button for **Reader Options.** This is the two As icon located at the right of the address bar.

- Then tap the smaller **A** to reduce text size and the bigger A to increase the text size.

How to Customize Favorites in Safari

Websites that you enjoy visiting should be added to your Favorites. This way, you can easily access them across all your Apple devices. Follow the steps below to do this:

- Launch Safari and navigate to the website you enjoy visiting.

- Move your pointer on the field for Smart Search.

- Tap **Favorites.**

How to Delete a Website from Favorite List

- Launch Safari and click on **Bookmarks** in the toolbar.

- Then tap **Show Favorites.**

- Locate the website you want to remove and right-click on it.

- Click **Delete** and the website would be deleted from your Favorites list.

How to Organize Safari Favorites

- Launch Safari and click on **Bookmarks** in the toolbar.
- Tap **Show Favorites**.
- Then drag the Favorite to its new location on the list.

How to Arrange Sites Under Frequently Visited

By default, sites that you visit are automatically added to your

Frequently visited list. You can choose to remove the sites whenever you want.

How to Access Your Frequently Visited Sites

- Launch Safari and click on **Bookmarks** in the toolbar.
- Tap **Show Favorites.**
- From that same screen, click on **"Show Frequently Visited in Favorites".**

How to Delete Frequently Visited Sites

- Launch Safari and navigate to the **Favorites** page.
- Under the section for Frequently Visited, you would see all the sites in this group.
- Right-click on the website you want to delete.
- Then click on **Delete.**

How to Access Siri Suggestions in macOS Catalina

The new software brought about Siri Suggestions on the start page of your Safari browser.

- Launch Safari and click on **Bookmarks** in the toolbar.
- Tap **Show Favorites**.
- Click on any link under Siri Suggestions.

Chapter 12: Conclusion

This book has extensively touched on all the important features of the macOS Catalina. The aim of writing this book is to ensure that you do not miss any detail that would help you to be productive when operating your computer.

If you are pleased with the content of this book, don't forget to recommend this book to a friend.

Thank you.